PETERBOROUGH
CATHEDRAL

The Revd. Canon Jack Higham

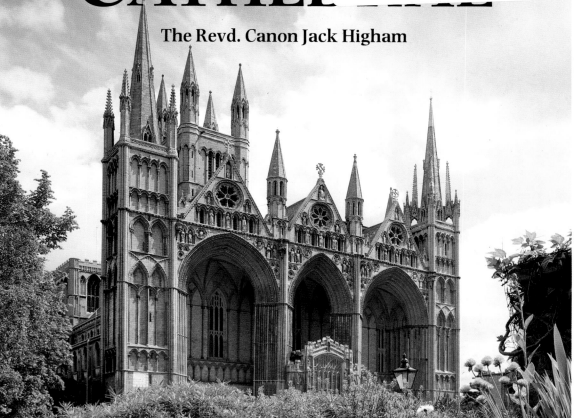

Contents

Above:
The West Front of Peterborough Cathedral which, with its three huge arches, is unique in Christendom.

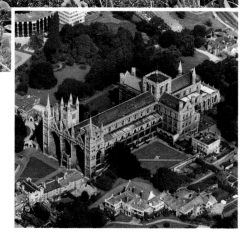

Right:
Aerial view of the cathedral and precincts.

History Chart

655 First abbey founded by Peada, king of Mercia.

870 First abbey sacked by the Danes.

960 Abbey refounded as a Benedictine House by Aethelwold, Bishop of Winchester.

970 or **972** Consecration of second abbey by Dunstan, Archbishop of Canterbury and Oswald, Archbishop of York in the presence of King Edgar.

*c.***1000** Defensive wall built around the abbey, making it a fortified place (a burgh) – hence, Peter's Burgh.

1116 Second church burnt in accidental fire.

1118 Present building begun at apse by Abbot John de Sais.

1140 or **1143** Consecration of eastern arm by Alexander, Bishop of Lincoln.

1145–55 Transepts and Norman tower by Abbot Martin de Bec.

1160–90 Nave by Abbots William of Waterville and Benedict.

*c.***1195–1230** West front in Early English style.

*c.***1220** Painted nave ceiling.

1238 Consecration of completed building by Robert Grosseteste, Bishop of Lincoln.

*c.***1335** Norman tower replaced by lower Decorated tower.

*c.***1380** Perpendicular porch and Chapel of the Holy Trinity (now the Treasury).

*c.***1400** Coffered wooden ceiling of presbytery.

1496–1508 New Building by John Wastell for Abbot Robert Kirkton.

1536 Burial of Katharine of Aragon.

1539 Dissolution.

1541 The former Abbey Church becomes the Cathedral of the newly created Diocese of Peterborough.

1587 Burial of Mary, Queen of Scots.

1643 Cathedral seized by Cromwell's soldiers. Destruction of stained glass, statuary, stalls and high altar.

1650s Cloister and Lady Chapel destroyed.

*c.***1860** Painted ceiling over apse by George Gilbert Scott.

1883–6 Central tower rebuilt.

1886–94 Cosmati marble floor, ciborium, Bishop's throne, pulpit and choir stalls by J. L. Pearson.

1896–1905 West front restored by J. L. Pearson and G. G. Bodley.

1949–75 New figures for west front by Alan Durst.

1975 Hanging nave rood. Cross by George Pace. Figure by Frank Roper.

1988 Major Appeal launched to mark the 750th anniversary of the consecration of the present building.

Dean's Welcome

Welcome to Peterborough Cathedral.

From the railway line and from the ring road, the huge sturdiness of the Norman structure makes its impact. Draw closer through the Norman Arch in Cathedral Square, and come into the forecourt; the majestic West Front inspires awe and wonder. Entrance into the Cathedral itself may bring the visitor into the spacious silence or the low murmur of visitors' conversation, or the musical splendour of worship.

This is the Cathedral of the City and Diocese of Peterborough. Peterborough is a new town, with a Cathedral 750 years old. Old and new have settled well together; and in this hallowed place Dean and Chapter are entrusted with the care and maintenance of the building, and the growth of spiritual life at the heart of the City. To do this, we have a small team of professional workers, and a large band of volunteers.

We all bid our visitors a hearty welcome, and pray that when you have looked and wondered in Peterborough Cathedral, you will resume your journey strengthened and inspired by God, our Creator and Sustainer.

THE DEAN

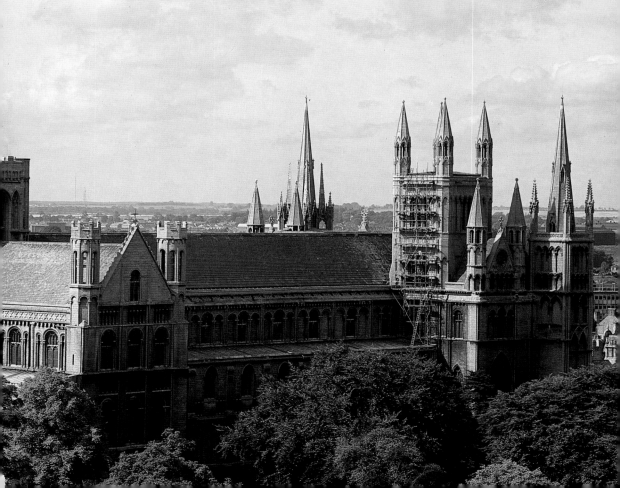

The First Abbey

The hanging rood in the nave declares: *Stat crux dum volvitur orbis*, 'The Cross stands while the earth revolves.' Those words, which are monastic in origin, stand as a witness both to the permanent value of the Christian faith and to the fact that despite Viking raids, accidental fires, local battles, Cromwell's soldiers and World War II bombers, this site has remained a place of prayer for over 1300 years.

For the first 900 years the church here was an abbey. According to Bede's 8th-century *History of the English Church and People* it was Saxulf, a Mercian nobleman, who founded the first abbey in 655, but the local chronicles name the founder as Peada, the first Christian king of Mercia, with Saxulf as the first abbot. The site was chosen probably because it was a good centre for communications, since one purpose of the foundation was

to evangelize the region. Six important monastic centres were founded from here in the 7th century: nearby Thorney, Repton in Derbyshire which still has a Saxon crypt, Breedon on the Hill in Leicestershire, where important early Saxon sculpture survives, Woking in Surrey, Bermondsey on the South bank of the Thames and Brixworth, Northants, which, as the finest 7th-century church surviving north of the Alps, no doubt gives a fairly accurate impression of what our first church looked like. This great work of evangelization is commemorated with a carved panel on the Victorian pulpit which shows Saxulf preaching the Gospel to the pagan Saxons of Mercia.

The first abbey here probably followed a Celtic pattern of monasticism, since the founders came from Northumbria, but while the church was being built a famous synod met at Whitby to decide whether Britain should follow the Celtic style of Christianity or that of Rome which Augustine had recently brought to Canterbury. The Roman order prevailed, and the coming of Deusdedit, Archbishop of Canterbury, to consecrate our first abbey in 665 was perhaps seen as a symbol of the union between the two, as well as a mark of the importance of the Abbey of Medeshamstede, as Peterborough was then known.

It was in 870 that Danish raiders came up through the Fens in their long ships and besieged the abbey. Villagers and monks all sought sanctuary in the great church, but the pagan Danes, who had no respect for Christianity, battered down the doors, slaughtered all whom they found, stole what they wanted and set fire to the rest. A monk of Crowland who came upon the site left a record that he had buried 84 monks, not counting villagers, which is a valuable indication of the importance of the monastery.

During restoration work in Victorian times, Saxon remains were discovered under the south transept of the present Cathedral, some of which may go back to the first abbey. Archaeological work has shown that the nave of the first church ran along the north half of what later became the cloister. The stone came from Barnack, and the 12th-century chronicler, Hugh Candidus, tells us that some blocks were so large that eight yoke of oxen could scarcely haul them. The Saxon remains may be visited by appointment. The only remains of the first abbey visible above ground level are the so-called Hedda Stone in the apse which shows Christ, the Blessed Virgin Mary and ten Apostles and was carved c.780, and the stone which shows two bishops in Phrygian caps doing a liturgical dance under a palm tree. This is dated c.800 and is to be seen on the west wall of the south transept. There is also a group of Saxon carvings in Fletton Church which may have come originally from our first abbey.

ST DUNSTAN

ST ETHELWOLD

Left: (13)
Stained glass (1958) in
St. Benedict's Chapel;
the founders of the
second abbey flanking
St. Benedict.

Below:
Carved woodwork of
choir stalls (c.1890), to
designs by Pearson.

The chroniclers tell us that for a hundred years the site lay in ruins, but they may have wanted to exaggerate the importance of the second foundation, and some modern historians argue that monastic life did continue at a much reduced level.

The story of the second foundation is told in the Victorian carved woodwork

on the west end of the north range of choir stalls. The upper scene shows Bishop Aethelwold of Winchester, who in his prayer is granted a vision of Christ who tells him to 'go unto the Middle Angles . . . and restore to its former state a certain ancient monastery of St. Peter'. Dutifully the good Bishop came here and found cattle and sheep grazing in the ruins of a once great church. On his return to Winchester, his prayers for the Lord's help were overheard by Queen Ethelfleda who suggested that he should seek her husband's support, as the centre bottom panel depicts. In the right-hand panel King Edgar is being shown a model of the proposed church by Aethelwold, while the left-hand panel recalls the consecration of the second abbey in 972 by Archbishop Dunstan of Canterbury and Archbishop Oswald of York, in the presence of King Edgar.

The involvement of both archbishops and the king (Alfred's great-grandson) reveals the importance of our great church, though what happened here was part of a general monastic revival in the 10th century, bringing back civilization to the areas devastated by the Danes. The modern glass (1958) by Carter Shapland in St. Benedict's Chapel in the south transept records the founding of the second abbey as a Benedictine house. In the centre light the founder of the order, St. Benedict of Nursia, reads the opening words of his famous Rule, by the power of which all the forces of evil are trampled down.

About the year 1000, a wall was built round the abbey as a defence work, which had the effect of changing the name to Burgh, 'a fortified place'; eventually the dedication of the church led to the name Burgh St. Peter, and finally Peterborough. Archaeologists have found traces of this original wall, and it is probable that the existing wall is built partly on the line of the Saxon one.

Oswald's Uncorrupted Arm

The 11th century saw a great interest in the cult of relics. Abbot Aelfsy (1006–55) was described as 'like a laborious bee' who 'stored his Abbey with them'. The prize possession was the uncorrupted arm of St. Oswald, the story of which is told in the Victorian woodcarving on the west end of the south range of the choir stalls. Bede recounts how Oswald, King of Northumbria, was always generous to the poor, and the top panel shows Oswald offering his own Easter dinner to the poor at his gates. Since there was not enough to feed them all, he ordered that his silver dishes be broken up, so that each poor person might have a little silver to buy food. His chaplain, St. Aidan, who is shown in the bottom centre panel, then took Oswald's right arm, declaring, 'May this arm which is so generous never perish.' Oswald himself was killed in battle at Oswestry in 642, but his right arm was miraculously preserved or perhaps mummified, as the right-hand panel depicts. The arm was kept at Bamburgh in Northumberland, but about 1060 a monk of Peterborough named Winegot somehow gained possession of the relic and brought it here to our abbey. The arm was the principal relic here until the Reformation when it was either destroyed or buried. The left-hand panel shows the story being told, and the Victorian sculptor has flattered the Dean of his day (Ingram) by giving the story-teller the Dean's face.

The cathedral still has a Chapel of St. Oswald in the south transept, which includes a rare example of a 12th-century watch tower where the horuspex, or monk of the watch, stood guard over the precious relic. The modern glass and reredos in this chapel also make references to Oswald's story, setting it in the context of other generous saints (Martin, Leonard and Crispin) and pointing to the love of the crucified Christ which 'constraineth us' (II Corinthians 5:14). Alan Durst's modern statue of King Oswald (complete with two arms) stands next to the present Queen high in the north arch of the west front.

Left:
Carved woodwork of choir stalls (c.1890), showing Oswald offering his Easter dinner to the poor.

Below: ⑬
Chapel of St. Oswald. Reredos by Bodley (1900) with (left to right) St. Oswald, Our Lord, St. Aidan. Oswald's arm was kept here until the Reformation.

Right:
Choir, crossing and
presbytery. Bishop's
throne and stalls by
Pearson (1890–94).
Original Norman arch
to transept, contrasting
with later pointed arch
to presbytery.

Below: ⑬
The 12th-century
watch tower in St.
Oswald's Chapel, in
which a monk stood
guard over the relic of
Oswald's arm.

The Norman Conquest

Abbot Leofric (1057–66), who is depicted as the fifth figure from the west on the south side of the choir stalls, was an eminent Saxon nobleman, nephew to his famous namesake of Coventry. He was present on Harold's side at the Battle of Hastings where he was wounded, dying a week later. The abbey, thinking William's victory was a flash in the pan, quickly elected another Saxon abbot, Brando (the fifth figure from the west on the north side of the choir stalls), who did homage to Edgar Atheling instead of William I, and soon had to pay William a large fine for his mistake.

When Brando died in 1069, William I quickly imposed a Norman abbot, Turoldus (the sixth figure from the west on the south side of the choir stalls), who came with 60 armed men to claim his abbey. There was a battle between Turoldus and Hereward the Wake (the sixth figure from the west on the north side of the choir stalls), which damaged the Saxon church and resulted in the temporary removal of Oswald's arm to Ely and then to Ramsey. It was when Turoldus threatened to burn down their abbey that the monks of Ramsey returned the relic. William I then imposed a very heavy tax requiring the abbey to provide 60 knights for the king's service, which was to remain a heavy burden on the abbey for a long period. The mound at the bottom of the Deanery Garden is a Norman motte erected by Turoldus, and still known as Tout (Turoldus') Hill.

Left:
Detail from north range of choir stalls, showing Hereward the Wake, by Pearson, 1892.

Below:
Detail of choir pulpit, by Pearson, 1892, showing Abbot John de Sais (1114–25) holding a model of the east end, which he started in 1118.

Left:
Exterior of Norman apse, begun in 1118. The windows were enlarged in the 14th century.

Far left: ⑪
South aisle, showing site of tomb of Mary, Queen of Scots. The four-part rib vaulting is, after Durham, the earliest in England.

The Third Abbey and Present Cathedral

It was on St. Oswald's Eve, 1116, that disaster struck. The medieval chronicler, who loves to moralize, records that Abbot John de Sais, momentarily enraged by the disobedience of his monks, told them they could all go to the Devil, while the monk in the kitchen, struggling to light the fire with a flint, cried out, 'The Devil take it', whereupon the Devil really did take his opportunity. He set fire not only to the kitchen but to the entire church, and a few days later sparks from the smouldering embers ignited the Abbot's Lodging too, which was only fair, since he had invoked the Devil in the first place.

Above: ⑥
Font. The bowl is 13th-century Alwalton marble and was recovered from a canon's garden in the 1820s. The supports are Victorian.

Below: ⑫
Saxon sculpture (c.800), discovered during Pearson's restoration, showing two bishops (or a bishop and a king) under a palm tree.

Left:
North transept (c.1150) from the south west. Note the varieties of Norman decoration – cushion capitals, alternating round and polygonal piers, billet moulding, roll moulding, zigzag and (within the tribune arches) imbricated patterns.

It is arguable that the fire was deliberately started as an excuse to replace an outmoded building that had been patched up after the Norman Conquest with one in the latest style. Certainly the disaster provided Abbot John with a glorious opportunity, and in March, 1118, he started work on the present building at the easternmost point of the apse. Memorial tablets to two 11th-century monks of Peterborough who had risen to become Archbishops of York were incorporated into the apse as foundation stones, where they can still be seen on the north side.

Abbot John knew that he could not possibly finish the task himself, but he built in faith, confident that others would see the work through to completion. In the end, it took eleven abbots and 120 years to finish the building. As with the earlier churches, the stone came from Barnack, which belonged to the abbey. A Victorian representation of Abbot John holding a model of the east end may be seen on the pulpit, but after only seven years' work he died. By 1140 the whole area east of the crossing had been completed and was consecrated by Alexander, Bishop of Lincoln, who made use of Oswald's arm in the ceremony. It is amongst the finest and purest Norman work in the country. The aisles use the rib-vaulting which had been invented at Durham only a few years before, and their walls are lined with intersecting blind arcading. The apse, despite being pierced by later Perpendicular work and despite the enlargement of the windows, still retains the atmosphere of high Romanesque, and is arguably the finest Norman apse in the country. The piers of the presbytery with their cushion capitals are twelve-sided, round and eight-sided, and there is much use of roll moulding, billet moulding and zigzag; indeed, Peterborough is the first known example of horizontal zigzag.

In the tympanum on the north tribune gallery are four circular holes which are perhaps an early development towards plate tracery. The roof of the presbytery is a later addition of *c.*1400, using wood in the manner of a stone vault. It has nearly 200 roof bosses of rather naïve workmanship. The ceiling over the apse, showing Christ and the Apostles, is by George Gilbert Scott and is based on descriptions of the medieval original, destroyed with musket fire by Cromwell's soldiers in 1643.

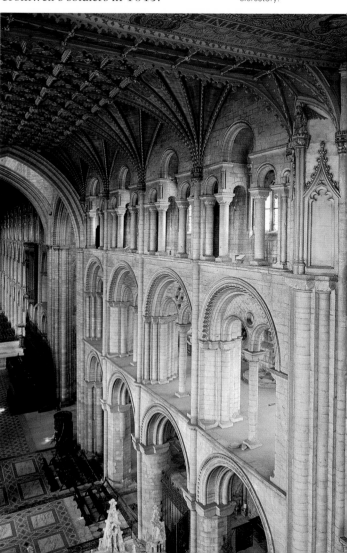

Right:
North transept (*c.*1150). Apart from the Perpendicular tracery, all the stonework is pure Norman and much of the wooden roof is original.

Below:
North wall of presbytery (1118–40) showing arcade, tribune and clerestory.

Left:
The great Norman nave (1160–85). Only since 1925 has the entire view been unimpeded by any form of screen.

Inset: Detail of Lamb of God on the painted wooden ceiling (c.1220). This ceiling is unique in England.

Above: ⑤
Sculpture (c.1200) in Alwalton marble at base of main doorway, showing Simon Magus being plunged into hell.

Below: ⑧
Effigy in Alwalton marble of Abbot Benedict (1177–93). The cathedral has the finest collection of Benedictine effigies in England.

The crossing and transepts were built by Abbots Martin de Bec (1133–55) and William of Waterville (1155–75), and are probably to be dated between 1145 and 1160. Apart from their tracery, most of the windows here retain their Norman shape, and the view from end to end of the transepts remains one of the most unspoilt Romanesque vistas in England. The wooden ceilings of the transepts, though restored in Victorian times, are partly original. Over the crossing there was originally a three-stage Norman tower which was probably similar to the existing tower of Norwich Cathedral, but the four piers supporting it were built only of facing stone with a rubble core. As the rubble settled, the upper parts became hollow and the tower became insecure. It was therefore replaced c.1335 with the present shorter tower and east and west crossing arches in the Decorated style, but the whole tower had to be rebuilt by Pearson, reusing the original stone, in 1883–6. The groined roof of the lantern tower was carefully restored by Pearson, who faithfully reproduced the work of 1335, with a central boss of our Lord, eight shields bearing emblems of the Passion and four symbols of the Evangelists.

The nave is largely the work of Abbot Benedict (1177–93), who came here from Canterbury, and whose remarkably well-preserved effigy in Alwalton marble may be seen in the north presbytery aisle. We owe him a great debt because he continued to build in the Norman style at a time when his former church of Canterbury was being rebuilt in the latest French Gothic. As a result we have a building of great purity, almost entirely Romanesque.

The painted wooden ceiling over the nave is one of the glories of the building. The work is of c.1220, and is totally without parallel in England, though there are three smaller painted wooden ceilings of about the same date on the Continent, in Germany, Switzerland and Sweden. The style owes much to manuscript decoration and Romanesque art. The fourth lozenge from the east in the centre row shows the Lamb of God; the fifth and seventh depict the Apostles Peter and Paul; between them is a running goat ridden backwards by a monkey holding an owl, all of which are medieval symbols of evil. The meaning is that the Lord has given His blood for our salvation which is preached by the Apostles in the midst of a wicked world. A 19th-century lithograph of the painted ceiling may be seen on a table in the north-west area of the nave.

The western transepts were built c.1200 and show an interesting mixture of Norman and Early English features. This is the only part of the building with a high vault in stone. The wooden doors are original. The sculpture in Alwalton marble at the base of the trumeau of the main doorway shows Simon Magus (Acts 8:9–24) who, according to a medieval legend, learnt to fly through his magical arts until his powers deserted him. He is depicted falling headlong to earth and being pushed on into hell by gleeful devils. This is intended as a contrast to Peter who holds the keys of heaven on the gable a hundred feet above – or rather, he did hold the keys until 1921 when, through the effects of erosion, he dropped them.

The west front is unique in Christendom in that it executes the Classical idea of a portico (compare the Parthenon) in Gothic style with huge originally free-standing piers supporting arches 85 feet high. There is evidence of several changes of plan during the development of this highly original design, in which number and musical symbolism are key features. Note how the central gable is made to rise to the same height as the others, despite springing from a narrower base. The three 13th-century figures at the top of the gables are Peter, Paul and Andrew, to whom the church is dedicated. Other statues are kings, apostles and individuals connected with the history of the building. Some are 13th-century figures, but others are modern replacements by Alan Durst. Two western towers were intended, but the fact that only the north one was completed (c.1270) gives the west front its asymmetrical appearance. The spires on top of the flanking turrets were added in the 14th century. Inside the gable behind the north-west turret is preserved an original windlass of c.1200, one of the earliest in England. It was used for hauling stone, and occasionally bells, to the upper levels of the west front, and its huge oak beam bears a deep groove worn by centuries of use.

The Perpendicular porch was inserted in 1380 to arrest the forward lean of the central arch, which can clearly be seen by standing at right angles to the west front. The roof bosses inside this porch portray in the outer bay the Coronation of the Virgin, and in the inner bay the Holy Trinity. Both are of high quality. The room over the porch was originally the Chapel of the Holy Trinity, but is now the Cathedral Treasury where church plate from all over the diocese is displayed.

The completed building, with the exception of the porch, was consecrated by

Left:
Windlass, or medieval winding machine (c.1200) in north-west tower. It stands over 10 feet (3 metres) high and was rotated by walking up the pegs.

Left: (9)
Rebus of Abbot Robert Kirkton (1496–1528) on frieze in New Building: A R followed by a kirk and a tun.

Below: (5)
Perpendicular porch (c.1380) inserted in central arch of West Front.

Above:
15th-century brass
eagle lectern made in
Tournai. Cromwell's
soldiers ripped off its
double branched
candlestick.

Right: ⑨
New Building (1496–
1508) with superb fan
vaulting by John
Wastell.

Below: ⑤
Roof boss of Holy
Trinity (c.1380) in inner
bay of porch.

Robert Grosseteste, Bishop of Lincoln in 1238. Shortly afterwards the nave windows were enlarged to five lights as we see them now. Before that the small Norman window openings such as may be seen in the north transept were unglazed and stuffed with twigs and straw. Decorated windows were inserted in the triforium and Perpendicular tracery was fitted into the clerestory windows.

A Lady Chapel was added on the north side to the east of the transept, c.1270, but it was damaged in the Civil War and pulled down c.1650. Traces of its west gable may be seen on the east side of the north transept outer wall. The fine brass lectern in the choir came almost cer-tainly from Tournai in Belgium, and is one of only about 40 medieval lecterns surviving in England. It was the gift of Abbot William Ramsey (1471–96) and Prior John Malden.

The last addition to the church was the New Building (1496–1508), east of the apse, by Abbot Robert Kirkton, whose rebus may be seen in several places, usually as A R followed by a church (kirk) and a barrel (tun). The architect was almost certainly John Wastell, who built the central tower of Canterbury Cathedral and King's College Chapel, Cambridge. The fan vaulting here is slightly earlier than his work at Cambridge and of equally high quality.

From Abbey to Cathedral

Abbot John Chambers, the last abbot, is the man to whom we owe the preservation of the building. He could see that the monasteries were about to be dissolved, and he therefore co-operated with Henry VIII's commissioners and cultivated friends in high places. As a result, when the greater abbeys were dissolved in 1539, Peterborough was one of the six that were chosen to be elevated to the rank of cathedral, and Henry's charter establishing the Dean and Chapter may be seen in the north aisle behind the choir stalls. The new diocese of Peterborough was actually established on 4th September 1541, being carved out of the huge diocese of Lincoln, and comprising Northamptonshire, Rutland and the Soke of Peterborough. (Leicestershire was added in 1839, but became a separate diocese in 1926.) John Chambers not only preserved the building but became the first bishop of the new diocese, the only abbot in the country to be so honoured. A poorly preserved effigy of him survives in the south side of the New Building.

Local tradition has often held that Katharine of Aragon also served to save the building. After her divorce from Henry VIII, she was moved away from the court and died at Kimbolton in 1536. Henry, wishing to save the expense of a funeral at St. Paul's, ordered that she be buried at Peterborough Abbey, where her body still rests in the north presbytery aisle. It is doubtful that Henry's plans for the church were influenced by sentiment for his first wife, but she is greatly honoured here, and hardly a day passes without fresh flowers on her grave. The standard of Henry VIII over her tomb was given by the present Queen, and that of Aragon, Castile and Leon by the Spanish Ambassador, with the addition of her personal emblem, the pomegranate (from the Spanish, *granada*), which recalls her happy childhood in Granada. The lettering marking her tomb was designed in 1986 by Alec Peever.

In 1587 another tragic queen was brought here for burial. Mary, Queen of Scots was beheaded at Fotheringhay in February of that year and after a long delay Elizabeth I ordered that her remains be buried here in the south presbytery aisle on 1st August, opposite Queen Katharine. Twenty-five years later Mary's son, James I, who had united England and Scotland, commanded that her body be removed to Westminster Abbey, opposite Elizabeth I. The gravedigger who buried both Queens was Robert Scarlett, whose portrait and wall painting may be seen on the west wall of the nave. During his long life, he claimed to have buried someone from every household in Peterborough twice over.

Right:
Charter of Henry VIII elevating Peterborough Abbey to a cathedral (1541).

Below: ⑪
Site of tomb of Mary, Queen of Scots. Her body now lies in Westminster Abbey. Note the fine ironwork (1894) by White & Son, London, in memory of Dean Argles (1891–93).

FORMER BURIAL PLACE OF
MARY QUEEN OF SCOTS

Right: ⑥
Portrait of Robert
Scarlett, the Elizabethan
grave-digger, on west
wall of nave. The dog-
whip in his belt and his
bunch of keys recall his
office as caretaker of
the parish church
(St. John's).

Left: ⑨
Effigy of John
Chambers, last abbot
(1528–39) and first
bishop (1541–56) of
Peterborough. Through
his friends at court, he
saved the building at
the Dissolution.

Left: ⑧
Tomb of Katharine of
Aragon, buried here on
29th January, 1536.
She lies beneath the
plain slab flush with the
floor.

Below: ⑬
Wooden panel
depicting seal of
Thomas Dove, Bishop
from 1600–30. This is
now the door to the
aumbry where the
sacrament is reserved.

The Civil War and After

In April 1643 a contingent of Parliamentary soldiers under Colonel Cromwell entered the cathedral and inflicted a great deal of damage. They destroyed all the stained glass, all the statuary, the choir stalls and the high altar; shortly afterwards the cloister was taken down to be used for building stone at Thorpe Hall. A few years later the lead and stone of the Lady Chapel were sold in order to raise funds for the repair of the main building.

As a result, the interior is uncluttered with monuments and the light streams in through clear glass, creating the purity which the Puritans were seeking. Some fragments of stained glass were collected together by Dean Tarrant in the 18th century and placed in the windows of the apse. The high quality of this glass underlines what a great loss the cathedral sustained. Amazingly, six effigies of abbots were spared destruction, probably because they were beneath the floor of the chapter house or under the high altar. They are now in the presbytery aisles and form the best series of Benedictine abbots in England.

The tapestries in the apse are Flemish, 17th-century, and depict two scenes from the life of St. Peter. They are clearly intended as a pair, linked by the theme of release from immobility. In one Peter heals the lame man in the Temple, while in the other it is Peter's own legs that are bound. The Lord's angel looses him from the chains, rescuing him from prison and imminent execution. In Acts 12:7, it is Peter's hands that are bound, so the artist has used his licence to make his point.

The best of the Victorian glass is the two-light window by Dante Gabriel Rossetti of the William Morris studios over the south transept door. It shows the sacrifice of Isaac and the rescue of Joseph from the well.

Left: ⑩
Detail of medieval stained glass in central window of apse, showing Peter and Our Lord.

Above: ⑬
Detail of window in St. Benedict's Chapel showing Humphrey Austin recovering the chronicle of the abbey from Henry Topcliffe, a Cromwellian soldier, for ten shillings in 1643.

Left:
Detail of Cosmati floor in presbytery by Pearson (1890).

Top right:
View of presbytery from tower, showing Pearson's elaborate marble floor and ciborium (1890–94).

Left: ⑫
Rossetti window (1862) in south transept.

In 1883 a large crack appeared in the masonry of the central tower, and J. L. Pearson's solution was to remove the tower completely, rebuild the four central piers, and then replace the tower with its original stones. He wanted to restore the east and west crossing arches to their original Norman shape (i.e. as they were prior to 1335), but a national controversy ensued, and the Archbishop of Canterbury (Benson) judged that the appearance immediately prior to the restoration work should be retained. Thus a marvellous opportunity of restoring a totally Romanesque appearance was lost. Pearson's great work of engineering took three years, in the course of which the stone screen east of the crossing was pulled down, creating an open vista from west end to high altar, though this was partially obscured by return stalls until 1925.

Pearson designed the elaborate Cosmati floor of the presbytery, executed in Italian marble, and his great ciborium over the high altar was inspired by that of Santa Maria in Cosmedin in Rome. The pillars are Italian marble, and the upper parts are Derbyshire alabaster. The four Evangelists stand at the corners supported by their symbols, while the Lord Christ looks straight down the church in blessing and Peter faces the apse. Pearson also designed the fine choir stalls, the pulpit and the *cathedra*, or Bishop's throne, all of which were executed by Thompsons of Peterborough.

The west front was partially restored by Pearson and Bodley at the turn of the century. Again there was national controversy and Pearson was accused of destroying a national treasure; the truth is that the national treasure would have fallen down without his intervention, and he reused as much of the original stonework as possible in a very careful and conservative work of restoration. The precious nave roof was twice pre-

served from German incendiary bombs by the vigilance of ARP wardens during World War II, and a fragment of a bomb is kept in a display case in the north west tower. The hanging rood in the nave was designed by George Pace in 1975. The figure of the Crucified Lord, in aluminium gilt, is by Frank Roper.

Above: ⑩
Ceiling over apse by George Gilbert Scott (*c.*1860), based on description of medieval ceiling destroyed by Cromwell's soldiers.

Above: ⑤
Treasury, displaying silver from many diocesan churches, housed over porch.

Right: ⑤
Two items from the Treasury, a 'Manus Dei' paten from Preston (c.1460) and a French crucifix paten from Dallington (1703).

Below: ④
Prior's Gate (c.1510), built by Abbot Robert Kirkton as the entrance to his deer park and plastered with devices to flatter the Tudors.

Above:
Detail of north arcade of ruined infirmary (c.1250). Some houses have been built into these ruins.

Below:
Central tower from the ruined cloister. The original Norman tower was replaced by the present Decorated structure (c.1335). The cloister was destroyed in 1643.

Above: ③
Sculpture (c.1300) of a mitred abbot on the Knights' Chamber. The Abbots of Peterborough sat in the House of Lords.

The Monastic Precincts

Only the outer walls of the great cloister remain, though the south wall preserves the lavatorium where the monks washed. The west wall of c.1100 is older than the cathedral church. To the south of the cloister was the refectory, traces of which remain in the Bishop's garden. There is a fine Norman chapel in the Bishop's Palace with modern glass by Patrick Reyntiens, and the entrance hall of the Palace includes 13th-century work from the Abbot's Lodging.

The dormitory has completely gone, but the passage beneath it is preserved in the walk south of the cloister, and at the southern end of this range of buildings is part of the misericord, or geriatric wing of the monastery. The infirmary was built c.1250 by Abbot John de Caleto, and the arches of its main building may be seen incorporated into houses to the south of the south transept. The drawing

room of one house was originally the Infirmary Chapel, and still preserves a double piscina. The Infirmarer's Hall is c.1250, while Table Hall is about two centuries later.

The Norman gateway from Cathedral Square is by Abbot Benedict c.1180, though it has been faced with Decorated work on the town side. There is a Norman Chapel of St. Nicholas on its upper floor. The building to the right as you come through the arch from the town incorporated the abbot's gaol, while the present Song School to the left is the chancel (1380) of the Chapel of St. Thomas à Becket which until the Reformation housed relics of Becket, brought by Abbot Benedict from Canterbury. The Norman nave of this chapel was taken down at the beginning of the 15th century when the Parish Church was being built across the road.

The Knights' Chamber is the building over the arch leading to the Bishop's Palace. This was built c.1300 and has six very fine original figures: Edward I, an abbot and a prior on the north side and Peter, Paul and Andrew on the south side. The Prior's Gate was built c.1510 by Abbot Robert Kirkton whose badly eroded rebus can still just be made out. He built it as the entrance to his own deer park, and he plastered it with symbols flattering the new Tudor dynasty.

The so-called Monks' Stables, to the south of the cloister, were probably originally the Almoner's Hall. In the main they are 14th-century work, and are being developed as a Visitors' Centre where visitors will learn about the history and life of this great church, once a Benedictine Abbey, and now a living cathedral where the faith has been maintained for over thirteen centuries and where worship and praise are offered daily to Almighty God through Jesus Christ our Lord.

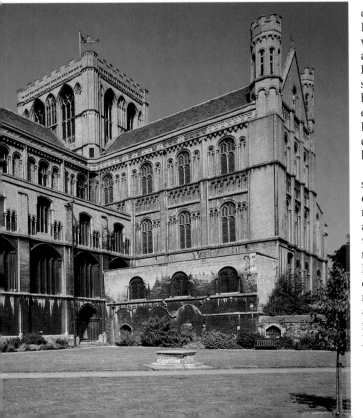